TOWARDS RECONCILIATION

By

Walter J. Burghardt, S.J.

1974
Publications Office
UNITED STATES CATHOLIC CONFERENCE
1312 Massachusetts Avenue, N.W.
Washington, D.C. 20005

Foreword

With the proclamation of a Holy Year of grace, Pope Paul expressed the hope that the year would "contribute to the tireless and loving effort of the Church to meet the moral needs of our time." To this end he has set for a theme that of Renewal and Reconciliation.

This theme speaks directly to the deepest needs of men and women today. Each of us stands in need of interior renewal. We stand in need of reconciliation with our God and with our fellow-pilgrims as we journey toward the Lord. Reconciliation has many other facets. It reaches to racial and ethnic groups, social and economic classes, areas of ecumenism and international relations.

In these pages Father Walter Burghardt illuminates the meaning of reconciliation in its many aspects. He does so with sensitivity and thought-provoking insight. To read his reflections is to take a first saving step toward the goals of the Holy Year. May God bless his efforts and give attentive listeners to his word.

TIMOTHY CARDINAL MANNING
Archbishop of Los Angeles
Chairman, Ad Hoc Committee on the
Holy Year, National Conference of
Catholic Bishops

About the Author

Father Walter J. Burghardt, S.J., is one of the country's best known theologians. He taught at Woodstock College from 1946 to 1974 and, effective September 1, 1974, is a member of the faculty of the School of Religious Studies, Catholic University of America. He is Editor of the journal *Theological Studies*, has written five books, and has lectured widely.

Contents

Preface

In its original form, the material in this booklet was presented on the NBC radio program *Guideline*—six addresses in January and February, 1974. Few changes have been made, and those are mostly stylistic. More importantly, the radio context affected the content. Inasmuch as the talks were directed to a broad audience, not simply to the Catholic constituency, I did not explicitly discuss certain facets of reconciliation which are part and parcel of the Catholic vision. Catholic readers, therefore, should broaden and deepen my presentation, move beyond my perspectives. Let them, for example, plumb the depths of the Eucharist as the sacrament par excellence of reconciliation, as well as the communal and more privately oriented celebrations of penance. No single booklet can do it all. I shall be content if I provide a provocative prologue and a useful framework.

WALTER J. BURGHARDT, S.J.

I
Who Needs Reconciliation?

In the autumn of 57, Saint Paul penned these enraptured lines to the Christians of Corinth: "If anyone is in Christ, he is a new creation; the old has passed away; behold, the new has come! All this is from God, who through Christ reconciled us to Himself and gave us the ministry of reconciliation. That is, God was in Christ reconciling the world to Himself, not counting their trespasses against them, and entrusting to us the message of reconciliation. So we are ambassadors for Christ, God making His appeal through us. We beseech you on behalf of Christ, be reconciled to God" (2 Cor 5:17-20).

On May ninth of 1973, Pope Paul proclaimed a Holy Year for 1975. For its inspiration, the Holy Year of Catholicism reaches back to the Jubilee Year of the Jews: the land rested, property was restored, slaves were freed. The distinctive theme for 1975, as Paul VI saw it, was frightfully urgent. He summed it up in Saint Paul's trumpet call: reconciliation.

To reconcile is to reunite, to bring back to harmony. Reconciliation implies, therefore, that division has taken place, separation, rupture. Two realities, two persons, two peoples are at odds, do not relate as they should. North Vietnamese and South Vietnamese, Christian and Jew, black and white, wife and husband— the examples are legion. There is discord, disunity, disharmony; oneness has been ruptured.

Four major ruptures call for reconciliation. These ruptures I shall analyze at fair length; but first I shall set the stage for the four acts to come, sketch the problem as one fairly fallible theologian sees it. I begin where we are, leap back to the beginning, move forward to the mid-point of history, return to today.

1.

If there is any one word that sums up the 70s, I suggest it is disunity. If there is any one characteristic that marks our present,

1

it is cleavage, conflict, division, disharmony. This absence of unity, of oneness—ultimately, of love—confronts us on four levels: between man and nature; within man himself; between man and man; between man and God.

In the first place, there is disunity, rupture, *between man and nature.* By "nature" I mean all that is not man or God. The problem is complex (as I shall detail later), but it has come to a focus, has come to haunt us, in ecology. The land we have ploughed and plundered, the chemicals that feed our life and heal us, the air we breathe and the ground we walk, the very wealth of our world threatens to strangle us. In consequence, it is more and more difficult to discover God in His creation, hard to touch God through the things of God. It is as though the things we see and hear and touch and taste and smell were divorced from the God who fashioned them—and, more frightening still, hostile to the men and women who use them. To survive this earth, we must subdue this earth.

Second, this disunity between man and nature is a symbol, and to some extent an effect, of the disunity that exists *within man himself.* I am one person, yet I am so often at war with myself. That deep-rooted conflict was described with rare insight by Saint Paul in his letter to the Christians of Rome: "My own actions bewilder me. What I do is not what I want to do; I do the very thing I hate. . . . It is not the good my will prefers, but the evil my will disapproves, that I find myself doing. In my inmost self I delight in God's law; but I see in my lower self another law at war with the law of my conscience, enslaving me to the law of sin which my lower self contains" (Rom 7:15-23). Even apart from sin, apart from the gentle Dr. Jekyll and the brutal Mr. Hyde, I am so often two persons, confused and confounded, tormented and distracted, unglued and unhinged.

Third, this disunity within man himself is a symbol, and to some extent a cause, of the disunity that prevails *between man and man.* Half the human race is at war with the other half. It is not simply a war between nations—Southeast Asia and the Middle East. A cold war rages between those who have and those who have not, between the powerful and the powerless, between employer and employee, between white and black, between atheist and believer, between Protestant and Catholic, even at times between a man and the woman who is one flesh with him. A terrifying feature of our times, from the human ashes in Dachau through the living corpses in Calcutta to the whispered words of hate in suburban New York, is "man's inhumanity to man." Like the pagans of Saint Paul's day, men and women whose law of life should be love have turned "ruthless, faithless, pitiless" (Rom 1:31).

Fourth, all these disunities—man and nature, man himself, man and man—are but a symptom, and in great measure an effect, of the most tragic disunity of all: the rupture *between man and God.* At this instant there are literally millions of men and women who say in their hearts "There is no God." There are millions more who say in their hearts "There is a God," yet exile Him effectively from their everyday living. And there are the uncounted millions whose experience of God is an experience of absence: God does not seem to be there. They simply do not find Him in crib or creation, on a cross or in His human images, in the proclaimed Word or "where two or three are gathered" in His name. He does not seem to be there.

2.

There you have the first significant fact: the fact of disunity. The second significant fact: disunity was not God's original design for us. However you interpret the first three chapters of Genesis— a real-life situation where human living originates, or inspired fiction with a religious message, or a wedding of both—the story of Adam and Eve reveals God's plan for human unity. Note the four levels on which the story moves.

In the first place, a remarkable oneness prevailed, an intimate harmony, *between man and God.* When God made the first man, He gave him not simply a garden of delights, the beasts of the field, the birds of the air, a woman from his flesh. More precious than all, God gave man God. The first instant Adam came from the hand of God, the first moment Eve was fashioned from the flesh of Adam, Father, Son, and Holy Spirit lived within them. Human creation was one with its Creator.

Second, there was a striking unity, a fascinating harmony, *within man himself:* within Adam, within Eve. That grim, unceasing struggle which we experience within ourselves, which Paul described—flesh warring against spirit, lust against love, passion

3

against purpose, all the schizophrenia that cleaves me into two—such conflict was foreign to Eden. Adam, like Eve, could not be seduced by surprise, could not say, as Paul would, "The very thing I hate, that is what I do." An inner poise, a sanity and serenity, a profound oneness, such was God's design; such was man to be.

Third, in God's plan a unique oneness would link *man with man*. In God's providence, the harmony within the flesh of Adam was symbolic of, was intended to flower in, an unbelievable harmony among his children till time was swallowed up in eternity. Never war, only peace; not hate, but love; no "mine and thine," only "I and thou."

A final unity God forged *between man and nature*. No sooner had He fashioned Adam and Eve to His own image, no sooner had He gifted them with the power to know and the freedom to love, than He blessed them, commanded them to create living reproductions of their life, commissioned them to touch the earth with their magic, link it to their love. In God's graciousness, mute creation would be eloquent; each "thing" would speak to man of the God who molded it. No starlight but would captivate his mind as it captivated Ignatius of Loyola; no rose but would ravish his soul as it ravished Teresa of Avila. At that moment each blade of grass, each feathered wing, each vein of gold, each breath of air was not a rival, not an enemy, not a reluctant captive, but a willing servant. And man looked on "things" with awe and delight, aware that God's Spirit moved over the face of the earth.

3.

There you have the second significant fact: God's design for human unity. The third significant fact: God's design was defaced, this primitive unity did not endure. Once again, the Book of Genesis raises more problems than it solves. But for our purposes one inescapable reality bursts into history. The disruptive element, the chaotic factor, is sin. And, as Genesis presents it, sin divided man; when Adam disobeyed God, he destroyed unity on four levels.

In the first place, Adam ruptured the bond that linked *man and God*. When love fled from Adam's soul, the God of love fled with it. The sentence in Genesis is expressive: "[God] drove out the man; and at the east of the garden of Eden He placed the cherubim, and a flaming sword which turned every way, to guard the way to the tree of life" (Gn 3:24). Man had been exiled from God.

Second, sin destroyed man's harmony *within himself*, the symmetry God had designed for every personality. Till the end of time, men and women would be dehumanized by the devil within them; man's worst enemy would be himself. For sin is schizophrenia, inward division: the one person at once image of God and image of Satan. Again, the words of Genesis after the first sin are pregnant: "The eyes of [the man and woman] were opened. . . . The Lord God called to the man . . . and [the man] said: 'I heard the sound of you in the garden, and I was afraid, because I was naked; and I hid myself' " (Gn 3:7-10). Man was a stranger to himself.

Third, sin severed the link God had forged *between man and man*, the link of love. In the wake of that primal sin, the first two brothers in the story of man went forth to a field, and (Scripture tells us) "Cain rose up against his brother Abel and killed him" (Gn 4:8). Man had been sundered from man.

Finally, sin shattered the oneness *between man and nature*. Material creation would conspire against him: the win and the waves would refuse to obey him, beauty would sedu. nim and loveliness betray him, animals would turn into enemies or slaves-by-compulsion. The promise God hurled at Adam is fraught with meaning: "Cursed is the ground because of you; in toil you shall eat of it all the days of your life" (Gn 3:17). And man, in his lust, would rape the earth to its destruction and possibly his.

4.

There you have the third significant fact: the fact of sin. But there is a fourth significant fact: the fact of grace. To restore the unity that had been sundered by sin, the Son of God became man. To recapture in some measure the divine dream of human harmony, to put man at peace with God, with himself, with his fellow man, and with all creation. God came to reconcile.

With His birth and His death Christ our Lord has destroyed the foundations of disunity; in Bethlehem and on Calvary God Himself began the task of reconciliation. To begin with, He linked man with God. "All those who welcomed Him He empowered to become children of God, all those who believe in His name" (Jn 1:12).

Second, He made it possible for man to live at peace with himself. Remember the problem of Paul? "Pitiable man that I am, who will set me free from a nature thus doomed to death?" Remember his answer? ". . . Jesus Christ our Lord" (Rom 7:24-25). Third, He made it possible for man to live at peace with his fellow man. "A new commandment I give to you, that you love one another as I have loved you" (Jn 13:34). To realize this love, He gathered us into one body, His own body, with Himself as Head: "You are all one in Christ Jesus" (Gal 3:28). Finally, He won for us the grace to live in some sort of harmony with material creation—not only with the animal but even with the atom. True, we cannot achieve that total, unlabored oneness which God originally intended between man and earth; but we can, with good will and God's grace, touch the earth and all its creatures with renewed reverence, conscious that the earth and its fulness are the Lord's, aware that we are not earth's despots but its stewards.

Such, I submit, are the broad outlines of a theology of reconciliation. Four critical ruptures: between God and man, within man himself, between man and man, between man and nature. Four ruptures that have their ultimate origin in man's sin, their ultimate reconciliation in God's grace. Four ruptures that call for careful, painful, prayerful analysis. I shall open the process by plumbing the basic rupture: *man severed from God*. As preparation, I would ask you to meditate the profound message of Saint Paul to the Colossians: "It pleased God that in [Jesus Christ] all the fulness of divinity should dwell, and through [Jesus] to reconcile to Himself all things, whether on earth or in heaven, making peace by the blood of His cross. And you, who once were estranged and hostile in mind, doing evil deeds, He has now reconciled in His body of flesh by His death, in order to present you holy and blameless and irreproachable before Him" (Col 1:19-22).

II

Reconciliation Between
God and Man

I open the process, the analysis, by plumbing the basic rupture: man severed from God. Here, as in so much that follows, I am talking about an uncomfortable monosyllable: I am talking about . . . sin. I do so without apology. And I do so with little embarrassment, if only because that remarkable psychiatrist Karl Menninger has just produced a heady volume entitled *Whatever Became of Sin?* (New York: Hawthorn, 1973). He is not afraid to speak of sin. He does not hesitate to quote the First Epistle of John (1:8): "If we say we have no sin, we deceive ourselves, and the truth is not in us." If a distinguished psychiatrist can confess the fact of sin, an undistinguished theologian dare do no less! I shall say something about the rupture that is sin—specifically how it ruptures man from God; and I shall suggest how man and God are reconciled.

1.

First, then, the rupture that is sin. What is this thing called sin? Let me begin with a strong statement from the Protestant theologian Paul Tillich: "Have the men of our time lost a feeling of the meaning of sin? Do they realize that sin does not mean an immoral act, that 'sin' should never be used in the plural, and that not our sins, but rather our *sin* is the great, all-pervading problem of our life? To be in the state of sin is to be in the state of separation. Separation may be from one's fellowmen, from one's own true self and/or from his God" (quoted by Menninger, *op. cit.,* pp. 189-90).

I do not agree with Tillich that "sin does not mean an immoral act"; at times it does and should. But it remains true that more important than any individual act of sinning is the state of sin,

7

and that this state of sin is a state of separation. Let me spell out these ideas—act, state, separation—from certain insights in the Old Testament, in the New Testament, and in contemporary theology.

In the Old Testament, to sin is not merely to miss the mark, to be deceived, to fall short of a goal; it is not only to be quite human, to fall short of what God and human persons have a right to expect of us. That is all very true; it is what we are all like— we all fall short; but this is altogether negative. Once Israel came to know God, sin was seen as rebellion. From the first man's sin to the whole nation's sin, to sin was to revolt, to rebel, to disobey. And the rebellion, though it could mean trampling on the rights of fellow humans, was at bottom and basically, ultimately and primarily rebellion against God: it meant deliberately, consciously, knowingly to resist the will of God, to flout His law. The first man sinned in that Adam ate of the tree "of which I commanded you, 'You shall not eat of it' " (Gn 3:17). David, adulterous murderer, finally recognized that he had not only violated the rights of Uriah: "I have sinned against *the Lord*" (2 Sam 12:13). And sin for the nation, for Israel, meant to play the harlot, to be unfaithful to God; it meant to break a covenant, to offend against a personal God.

In the Hebrew tradition *all* men were sinners. That tradition was pithily expressed by the preacher we know as Ecclesiastes in the third century before Christ: "there is no man on earth so just as to do good and never sin" (Eccl 7:20).

The New Testament builds on the Old. Here Luke, Paul, and John are especially insightful. St. Luke's parable of the prodigal son suggests vividly what it really means to sin. To sin, as the prodigal sinned, is not primarily to squander a father's wealth; to fornicate, as the prodigal fornicated, is no more than a symptom of something more profound. To sin is to break a bond, to destroy a relationship, to withdraw *myself* from God my Father and from His love. The words of the prodigal are pregnant: "Father, I have sinned against heaven and before you; I am no longer worthy to be called your son" (Lk 15:18). This is what the elder brother failed to understand. Angrily he assailed his father: "Look, these many years I have never once disobeyed a command of yours" (Lk 16:29). Important yes, but not all-important.

St. Paul tells us of a "sin" that is almost a personal force. It indeed entered the world through one man's rebellion, Adam's act of disobedience. But it is more than a single act: it is an evil force, a malevolent power, that tyrannizes every man born into this world. It is a power hostile to God, a power that alienates men from God. Its works are sinful deeds. Because of it, Paul says, "I do not do the good I want, but the evil I do not want" (Rom 7:19). It is Sin with a capital S.

For St. John, sin is separation from God. For sin implies that the sinner is enslaved to the devil, that he dwells in darkness, that he is spiritually dead. Sin is the hostility of a man or woman against a God who would save them. Sin, for John, has a frightful facet: I hate God.

Rebellion against God, hostility to God, alienation from God, destruction of covenant between man and God—these biblical insights into sin theologians are constantly trying to recapture, to organize, to deepen. Four aspects of this theology of sin can be uncommonly fruitful. First, a sin is not merely an individual act about a particular object: I robbed a friend of fifty dollars, I had lustful desires about a woman, I told a needless lie, I shredded a rival's reputation, I killed an enemy in cold blood. These are indeed "sins": I have introduced moral disorder into the world. More importantly, in sinning I am realizing myself as a person; these acts express, give the shape of, who I am. Not always; not any isolated act. It is one thing to tell a lie, another thing to be a liar; one thing to kill, another thing to be a killer. And still it remains true that a sinful act is less important for the disorder it creates than for what it says about me as a person: Who am I? Whom do I love? What is my attitude towards God?

Second, there are situations in life where I am not so much master of my freedom, not so fully aware of myself as a person, that my actions, my sins, engage me as a whole person. In a sense, I say no to God, but not so totally that I cease to love Him. It is not a fully personal no. I do not close myself to God. Call it venial sin, slight sin, even serious sin—whatever you will: it is not the inner core of me that rebels. I do not break the bond that links me to God. The love relationship abides.

Third, there are other sin situations where I commit myself completely as a person. I am aware of God inviting me to communion with Him; I sense that what I say or do here is crucially important; I am remarkably, thrillingly free—and I say no. It is

9

Adam deciding that he will be as God is; it is David taking Bathsheba and murdering Uriah; it is the prodigal son cutting himself off from his father; it is Judas sacrificing his Saviour for silver; it is Pilate washing his hands of the Christ in whom he finds no crime; it is perhaps Peter swearing by God that he does not know the Man. This is sin at its most profound, because it is my total self that rebels. Mortal, because it is sin unto death. Not perhaps the ultimate rebellion (take Peter or the prodigal), but perilously so (take Judas). Perilously so because in such sin *I* sin, this total person, free and unfettered. Perilously so, because this sort of sin is what makes me genuinely a sinner. Perilously so, because a covenant has been crushed and I am a stranger to God. How often I say no with such freedom and finality, not even a Jesuit can say. I would think, rarely, because "a life which can in short hops go from life to death, then back again to life, and then to death is not life at all" (John W. Glaser, S.J., "Transition between Grace and Sin: Fresh Perspectives," *Theological Studies* 29 [1968] 262).

Fourth, such sin stems from what the Gospel of John calls "the sin of the world" (Jn 1:29), the virus of evil that entered the world (Paul says) "through one man" (Rom 5:12), that "dynamically unfolds itself and tightens its grip on humanity and on the world in an escalating fashion down the ages of history. It is the hidden power which multiplies transgressions in the history of mankind. They are merely its symptoms; it is greater and deeper than all of them" (Kevin F. O'Shea, C.SS.R., "The Reality of Sin: A Theological and Pastoral Critique," *Theological Studies* 29 [1968] 244).

2.

Sin, then, is profoundly a matter of man and God; and at its worst, sin ruptures man from God. I admit, it is the rare sin that assaults God directly; few humans curse God with utmost serious-ness. Most sins are leveled at the image of God: another human person. And still, each sin touches the divine: the covenant, the link, that relates earth to heaven.

Rupture between man and God calls for reconciliation between man and God. And because the rupture that is mortal sin, sin unto death, is rebellion, hostility, alienation, destruction of a covenant, it will not do to simply say "O my God, I am heartily sorry for having offended thee." Reconciliation calls for conversion. For

10

only conversion reverses the radical rupture that sin creates. Like sin, conversion means that my whole person changes: I have a new stance towards God, a new way of looking and living; I change the whole thrust of my life. No single cry of sorrow, no one act of love, will do this. *I* must change. I must give to God a total yes that is expressive of *me*.

The problem is, I cannot change myself. There is a paradox here: I can turn *from* God all by myself; I cannot turn *to* Him all by myself. St. Paul said it pointedly to the Christians of Corinth: "All this is from God, who through Christ reconciled us to Himself . . . ; that is, God was in Christ reconciling the world to Himself. . . . For our sake He made Him to be sin who knew no sin, so that in Him we might become the righteousness of God" (2 Cor 5:18-21).

"In Him. . . ." Reconciliation, conversion, comes through Christ. It began in Bethlehem, where a new oneness, a root unity, between God and man was born. For the flesh that God took is our flesh: in some genuine sense, it is my flesh, your flesh, the flesh of every human person born into this world. The Son of God became what we are, that we might become what He is. In Bethlehem forgiveness was born, a new covenant. Reconciliation climaxed on Calvary, where "the sin of the world," the tyrannizing power that has torn man from God since the beginning, was leveled in the blood of Christ. And reconciliation touches each of you now in the risen Christ, who offers you time and again a new covenant with God and makes it possible for you to respond with a total yes.

Conversion . . . to Christ . . . through Christ. I am not suggesting that at this moment you are turned totally from God and His Christ, alienated from God, in rebellion against Him, that you have not experienced conversion, that you are in a state of sin. Quite the contrary. My experience of Christians is very much my experience of myself: turned radically to Christ in mind and will, but dreadfully weak in living the logic of that conversion. You cannot call me sinner, because my face is set towards Christ. But you can call me sinful, because so many of the actions that should express who I am, a committed lover of Christ, give the lie to that person. So much of my life is superficial. I mean, so many of my human acts are not fully human, do not commit me as a total person. They are neither sin in the radical sense nor con-

11

version. They do not enslave me to Satan, they do not commit me to Christ. The danger in such semi-Christian living was strongly stated in the last book of the Bible: "I know your works: you are neither cold nor hot. Would that you were cold or hot! So, because you are lukewarm, and neither cold nor hot, I will vomit you out of my mouth" (Ap 3:15-16).

I have asked you to take a fresh look at the rupture that is sin, a fresh look at the reconciliation that is conversion. I have insisted that both rupture and reconciliation involve a relationship of man with God. I have suggested that, to grasp this relationship, you look less at your individual sins, more at the sort of person these sins express; look less at your endless acts of contrition, more at the kind of person such remorse images. I have argued that mortal sin, sin unto death, total alienation from God, is rare among earth's men and women; but I have hinted at the peril that over-hangs those whose face indeed is Godward but whose hands and hearts are earth-bound.

I conclude these reflections with St. Paul's message to the Colossians: "And you, who once were estranged and hostile in mind, doing evil deeds, He has now reconciled in His body of flesh by His death, in order to present you holy and blameless and irreproachable before Him, provided that you continue in the faith, stable and steadfast, not shifting from the hope of the gospel which you heard . . ." (Col 1:21-23).

III

Reconciliation Within Man Himself

In St. Paul's letter to the Christians of Rome there is a remarkable chapter in which the Apostle reveals his inner conflict, the rupture that rends him within, the schizophrenia that makes two persons of him: "I do not understand my own actions. For I do not do what I want, but I do the very thing I hate. . . . It is no longer I that do it, but sin which dwells within me. For I know that nothing good dwells within me, that is, in my flesh. I can will what is right, but I cannot do it. For I do not do the good I want, but the evil I do not want is what I do. Now if I do what I do not want, it is no longer I that do it, but sin which dwells within me. So I find it to be a law that when I want to do right, evil lies close at hand. For I delight in the law of God, in my inmost self, but I see in my members another law at war with the law of my mind and making me captive to the law of sin which dwells in my members. Wretched man that I am! Who will deliver me from this body of death?" (Rom 7:15-24).

To this point I have argued that sin is rupture, that the radical rupture rends man from God; for sin is rebellion against God, hostility to God, alienation from God, destruction of covenant between man and God. Reconciliation, therefore, is an empty six-syllable word unless unity, harmony, oneness is restored between man and God; but peace between man and God is not the work of man, it is the love of Christ. Now I shall argue that the schizophrenia of sin not only severs me from God; it ruptures me within, makes two persons of me, two persons at war. And I shall insist that reconciliation, the destruction of sin's inner rupture, is a chimera, sheer whistling in the dark, apart from St. Paul's response: "Who will deliver me? God, through Jesus Christ our Lord" (Rom 7:24-25).

First, then, sin is schizophrenia. I am not using schizophrenia as a psychiatrist would. I am not suggesting that the sinner is psychotic, that he has lost contact with his environment, that his personality has disintegrated, that he needs a psychiatrist. I mean, to be a sinner is to be schizoid in its root sense: in sin I am inwardly divided, I am not the one person God shaped me to be.

Frightfully abstract? I suspect so. To concretize it, I suggest we go back to the early centuries of the Christian era, to those theologians we call "Fathers of the Church" because they fashioned the spiritual personality of the ages to come. The Fathers rang the changes on a favorite theme, a sentence from the first page of Scripture: "God created man in His own image, in the image of God He created him; male and female He created them" (Gn 1:27). What does it mean to image God? With basic help from Scripture, and some misunderstanding of the biblical witness, the Fathers constructed a number of image theories, not always in harmony one with another. But on one fundamental facet they were all at one: the model for our imaging of God is the Man who is Image with a capital I: God's Son in flesh. He is God's perfect likeness—at once God's blinding revelation of Himself and God's clarifying revelation of what we should be. In fact, as far back as the second century, the first Christian theologian, Bishop Irenaeus of Lyons, claimed that the first man to be made, Adam, was made not simply "in the image of God," but in the image of Christ to come. Even then, at the dawn of human creation, Christ was all-important in God's plan for man. Not as an afterthought, an appendage, an epilogue, a remedy for sin. No. Even apart from sin, as Irenaeus seems to have sensed it, God would have come to us in human flesh, because even apart from sin He was the model for our humanness.

That is why, Irenaeus proclaims, the first man was fashioned as he was: not only human flesh and human spirit, but flesh and spirit made genuinely human because pervaded and transformed by the Spirit of God, the Holy Spirit. This was the first man because this was to be the Second Man; this was Adam because this was to be Christ.

Here you have man at his most human, his most Christlike: man strikingly one, not only with God but within himself, because ruled by the principle of oneness, the Holy Spirit. Flesh in harmony with spirit, spirit in harmony with Holy Spirit. Sin ruptures that one-ness—the very first sin and every sin where my whole free self rebels. Sin ruptures my oneness because the Holy Spirit is no longer there and I am at war with myself. In St. Paul's terms, "I do not do what I want, I do the very thing I hate. . . . I can will what is right, I cannot do it."

The Fathers of the Church saw this problem of sin-as-rupture in terms of man-as-image. Many of them were puzzled: Does sin destroy God's image in man, or disfigure it? Obliterate it utterly, or merely mar it? The problem is not artificial. On the one hand, the Holy Spirit is no longer within me; I am not now Spirit-led, I am Spiritless; and so I am no longer Christlike, no longer the image of God a Christian ought to be. On the other hand, sin, for all its destructive power, cannot so loose the bonds which link man to God that sinful man is simply Godless. The third-century theologian Origen saw this acutely and expressed it vividly: "It is the Son of God who painted [the image of the heavenly] on man. And because the painter is so remarkable, His image can be obscured . . . , it cannot be destroyed . . . ; for it remains always the image of God, even though you may put over it the image of the earthy" (*Homily 13 on Genesis* 4). The point is: even severed from God, the sinner belongs to God; despite his no to God, God still calls to him; earth-bound in fact, he is Godward in destiny.

Precisely here lies sin's schizophrenia: I am inwardly split, torn, rent. In day-to-day living, I am no longer linked to God by love; I have shouted a rebellious, definitive, covenant-rupturing no to Him. And at the same time my whole person cries out for Him. Silently yes, mutely indeed; but none the less really. More tragic because unrecognized; a more profound frustration because only my rebellion is audible, and the core cry of my heart for my God is muted within the depths of who I am.

This is when sin cuts most sharply, splits the Christian person in two: when my response to the covenant call of a loving God is an absolute no that stems from my total self in complete freedom. But this sort of rejection is hardly our everyday experience. My own schizophrenia, I suspect, parallels the experience of most Christians. I do not hurl at God a definitive no; I do not really reject Him; at bottom, when all is said and done, I love Him; and

15

so, in harmony with the promise of Christ, God loves me and lives within me: Father, Son, and Holy Spirit are tabernacled in me. But I do not live out the logic of that dynamic divine presence; I play games with God. I neither embrace Him totally nor repulse Him completely—and that is a dangerous line to walk, a perilous tightrope.

It was the ceaseless sin of the Israelites as denounced by the Lord through Jeremiah: "You have played the harlot with many lovers; and would you return to me?" (Jer 3:1). It is the recurring sin of Christians whenever we try to serve two masters. I compromise. I crawl to the edge of sin-unto-death . . . but not quite over. And so you have that endless catalog of "venial" sins— I disobeyed, I lied, I gossiped, I cursed, I got angry, I drank too much, I stole—repeated so often that I question my own sincerity. You have that smaller list of "serious" sins—from lust for another's flesh to lust for another's life—which are not "unto death" for me only because I did not quite know what I was doing. And most importantly, you have that set of sins impossible to catalog—sins of "omission"—impossible to catalog because in each instance I did . . . nothing. A child was starving, and I closed my eyes; napalm fired human flesh, and I said nothing; public officials betrayed their sacred trust, and I thought "Everybody does it"; a stranger asked a smile, and I never gave it.

Christian schizophrenia as I see it, sin's inner rupture as I experience it, is rarely a clear no to a God who will not let me go. Rather, I am rent within, inwardly divided, because I compromise, come to terms with two masters, do not live the Life that burns and yearns within me.

2.

But if such is sin's inner rupturing, whence comes reconciliation? How can I be made whole again? The basic answer is St. Paul's glad cry: "Who will deliver me? God, through Jesus Christ our Lord" (Rom 7:24-25). The problem is, Jesus Christ is not a magic formula: you speak His name and there He is; you wave your hand and you are healed by Him.

And yet the Christian paradox lies precisely in this: Jesus Christ *is* there! Take the most radical form of sin's schizophrenia—where I have shouted a definitive no to God, where my living actions, at once cold-blooded and passionate, have declared that *I* am supremely important, not God. Indeed I am no longer linked to God by love; Father, Son, and Spirit no longer live in me. Nonetheless, I cannot sever the last strand that binds me to divinity: like it or not, want it or not, I am God's; and so God and His Christ constantly call to me, will never cease calling till I murmur a no in death which is beyond recall. Put another way: I may stop loving Christ; He never stops loving me. The proof has to be Calvary. As St. Paul summed it up: "If while we were enemies we were reconciled to God by the death of His Son, much more, now that we are reconciled, shall we be saved by His life" (Rom 5:10). No matter how deep that divisive rupture, the Son of God is there to heal it.

But again, I am not so much interested in this radical rupture which ends love, this radical reconciliation which demands a fresh beginning—almost like Calvary all over again. What I called our everyday experience, the day-to-day rupturing—the casual "small" sins and the thoughtless 'big" sins and the mass of omissions— this is where reconciliation must touch your daily existence. Here is where you grow into one person or split insensibly into two. The Spirit of Love lives in you, the source of reconciliation, of inner oneness, of harmony between flesh and spirit, between the spirit of man and the Spirit of God—what must you do to free Him for reconciling action within you?

Aye, there's the rub! To free Him. . . . My obstacle, after half a century, is not God, not the world's men and women; my obstacle is myself. It is a strange and disturbing fact: the more I focus on myself, the more divided I am inside. The more selfish I am, the less of a single self I am. Not strange at all, if I reflect a bit. St. Augustine's oft-quoted confession has been quoted so often it has lost its savor: "Thou hast made us for thyself, O Lord, and our heart is restless till it rests in thee." And modern philosophers join contemporary youth in insisting that I am authentically a person, a self, to the extent that I am "for others." For God, for others: only by moving outside myself can I become genuinely myself, a person, a wholeness.

To be at peace within, therefore, to reconcile the conflicting forces inside of me, I must deaden this damnable, distressing stress on myself—on *my* needs and *my* wants, on *my* self-fulfilment and what is meaningful to *me*. I must let the Spirit lead me

17

where He will. A perilous resolve, replete with risk—once I remove that resolve from the safe order of the abstract. For I do not know where the Spirit might lead me if I let Him; and at times I am not at all sure it is the *Holy* Spirit who has taken the reins. But the blessing of it is that the Spirit will lead me outside myself, lead me to "the others," those who are less human because I am less Christian: to the child of six who has never heard a word of love, and the lonely old lady whom everyone shuns; to those who hate me because I seem to have so much, and those who pity me because I seem to live so little; to all those in search of something to live for, those in sorrow over life that has died. These "others" are legion; but only through them will I escape that small self in whose womb so much sinfulness comes to birth. And in leading me to "the others," the Spirit will be leading me to "the Other"; for, as the Jewish philosopher Martin Buber emphasized, every individual thou is a reflection of the eternal Thou. Only in Him will all our inner ruptures ultimately be reconciled, and we shall stand forth images of Christ alone, images of nothing else created.

IV

Reconciliation Between Man and Man

In the First Epistle of John there is a terrifyingly strong paragraph: "This is the message which you have heard from the beginning, that we should love one another, and not be like Cain, who was of the Evil One and murdered his brother. And why did he murder him? Because his own deeds were evil and his brother's righteous. . . . We know that we have passed out of death into life, because we love our brothers and sisters. He who does not love remains in death. Anyone who hates his brother is a murderer, and you know that no murderer has eternal life abiding in him. By this we know love, that [Jesus] laid down His life for us; and we ought to lay down our lives for our brothers and sisters. But if anyone has the world's goods and sees his brother in need, yet closes his heart against him, how does God's love abide in him? Little children, let us not love in word or speech but in deed and in truth" (1 Jn 3:11-18).

Thus far I have argued that reconciliation implies rupture: oneness has been destroyed. I have argued that ultimately rupture has its origin in sin, finds its reconciliation in God's grace. I have insisted, first, that the radical rupture rends man from God. I have insisted, second, that the schizophrenia of sin ruptures me within. Now I shall discuss a third rupture that is the work of sin. I shall argue that sin severs man from man, human person from human person. And I shall insist that reconciliation, the destruction of sin, the restoration of oneness among God's children, is impossible unless love lays hold of us, unless we lay hold of God in love, lay hold of man in love. The "two great commandments of the law" are really one: I cannot love God if I hate my neighbor, and I will not love my neighbor as I should unless I love God with all my mind and heart, with all my soul and strength.

First, then, sin severs man from man. You see, few sins are aimed directly at God. Rarely does a human being set up what he knows are false gods; rarely does he curse God in cold blood. More often I sin by offending against the image of God: I sin against man. Most sins reflect the sin of Cain, who turned on his brother Abel and slew him. Most sins exemplify man's inhumanity to man.

Some of this inhumanity has taken place on a scale so vast, on a canvas so broad, that you cannot grasp it if you live or die outside it. I am thinking of the gigantic inhumanities man has inflicted on man just in my lifetime. Take war and politics. Two world wars: the first took 10 million lives, the second took 15 million in military personnel alone. Two atomic bombs fashioned a new hell in Hiroshima and Nagasaki. Nazi gas chambers exterminated six million Jews. Aleksandr Solzhenitsyn's explosive book tells of 12 million Russians in any given year imprisoned, tortured, or killed in the network of prison islands he calls the Gulag Archipelago. The Spanish Civil War cost a million lives. Napalm converted Vietnam into family incinerators. Nine and a half million refugees clogged the roads of East Pakistan. Terrorist bombs maimed women and children in Northern Ireland, and a blockade threatened millions with starvation in Biafra. All this and much more in my short span of living.

Take poverty. Each night two out of every five human persons on this earth go to bed hungry—two out of five. One third to one half of the human race suffers from nutritional deprivation. The United States, with 6 percent of the earth's population, controls 40 percent of the earth's wealth. The North Atlantic nations, with 16 percent of the earth's peoples, control 80 percent of the earth's wealth. And if those figures seem abstract to you, here is how many years you could expect to live if you grew up in certain other countries: Cambodia, 44; Kenya, 43; Burma, 42; Sudan, 40; Ghana, 39; Madagascar, 38; Libya, 37; Cameroon, 36; South Vietnam, 35; Togo, 34; Chad, 32; Syria, 30 to 40; Nepal, 25 to 40. And beneath these naked figures smolders a volcano of envy and resentment, of frustration and hate. For if war is sinful because man does something—something evil, poverty is sinful because man does nothing.

Take race: black and white in South Africa, black and white in the United States. In our own "land of the free" I have seen the subtle, bloodless violence of white power—power that enslaved a whole race, condemned it to ghettos and the back of a bus, forced it to study in shacks and work in toilets, forbade it our sidewalks and our pews, barred it from hotels and restaurants, from movie houses and rest rooms. Not because these people were ignorant or dirty or penniless; only because they were black. And they won their freedom not because the master race loved them; they forced freedom from us by their blood and our law. A court of law proved more powerful than the Sermon on the Mount. In consequence, you have the black reaction: in large measure they despise us, hate us. So much so that a prominent black theologian has confronted white Christianity with these harsh words: "[We have] no use for a God who loves whites the *same* as blacks. We have had too much of white love, the love that tells blacks to turn the other cheek and go the second mile. What we need is the divine love as expressed in Black Power, which is the power of black people to destroy their oppressors, here and now, by any means at their disposal" (James Cone, *A Black Theology of Liberation* [Philadelphia: Lippincott, 1970] p. 132).

War, poverty, race—here is the legacy of Cain on national, global, cosmic levels. But the rupture between man and man is not something that begins "out there" somewhere. If, as Isaiah proclaimed, "peace is the fruit of righteousness" (Is 32:17), if, as the Second Vatican Council taught, "peace is likewise the fruit of love" (*Gaudium et spes*, no. 78), then war is the fruit of unrighteousness, of hate. But I dare not lay that unrighteousness, that hate, solely at the feet of the enemy, only in the heart of the politician, blame it all on the dictators of our day. If I am as honest as I want my neighbor to be, I must look within, to see if the seeds of war are planted in my heart. I dare not be less Christian than Christ demanded when He said: "You have heard that it was said to the men of old, 'You shall not kill, and whoever kills shall be liable to judgment.' But I say to you that whoever is angry with his brother shall be liable to judgment; whoever insults his brother shall be liable to the council; and whoever says 'You fool!' shall be liable to the hell of fire" (Mt 5:21-22).

Granted that poverty and malnutrition, infant mortality and early old age, are complex issues, far beyond the power of any

21

one individual or group to resolve. It still remains true that people are dying as they are because we are living as we are. Whole cities could live on the garbage from our dumps, on the clothes we wear once, on the luxuries we have made necessities. We dare not lay the blame on "the nation"; the nation is "we the people." As with war, so with poverty, I must look into my heart and ask: Is someone in agony, across the street or across the world, because I do not care enough?

So too with race. Never have I spoken harshly to a black man; but never have I spoken harshly to an American Indian either! Before I absolve myself of all responsibility for the hatred that severs white and black, I must ask myself several questions: Does the comfort I enjoy—house, food, job, money—stem in any way from America's long history of exploitation, of injustice to a whole race? How often have I taken the first step towards a black person, to ease his hunger not so much for food and drink as for understanding and love—to lift a little of his loneliness, his feeling that he was not wanted? Do I share the conviction of many Christians that "the whole thing has gone too far," that "they" are getting far more than they merit? Can I say honestly that I love them as human persons fashioned by God in His image and refashioned in the blood of Christ?

2.

This brings me to my second point: How in the concrete can the rupture be healed, how can man be reconciled to man, how can I become a force for reconciliation? From one perspective, the task seems hopeless. Will anything anybody does heal the hatred that inflames Northern Ireland and West Africa, Southeast Asia and the Middle East? Is it realistic to think we can feed and house and clothe a world population that is now doubling every thirty-five years? Can we expect more than an armed neutrality between black and white in the United States?

The total task may be hopeless, and still we are not helpless. I shall not pre-empt the order of politics; my purposes are pastoral. Let me suggest several Christian responses to the sins that sever man from man.

A first step to reconciliation is to . . . remember. That remarkable Jewish storyteller Elie Wiesel, who feels guilty because he survived the Holocaust, tells us that, for Jews, to forget is "a crime against memory as well as against justice: whoever forgets becomes the executioner's accomplice" (*The Oath* [New York: Random House, 1971]). It is too convenient for Christians to forget that the Holocaust took place in a Christian country, too easy for us to say "I wasn't there," too simple to shrug our shoulders and wash our hands of it. Time erases bad memories— except for the Jews; for all too many of them, God died in Auschwitz. And time erases what I have done to my fellow man, or failed to do for him. I am not asking you to brood, to become neurotic, to fasten sickeningly on your failures. I am asking you simply to remember. Don't become "the executioner's accomplice."

But remembrance is not enough. Sin calls for sorrow—even where it is not I who have sinned, but the Christian community of days long gone. One example. Thoughtful Jews who welcomed Vatican II's Declaration on Non-Christian Religions, who welcomed the Church's rejection of the "Christ-killer" canard, were bewildered by the absence "of any note of contrition or repentance for the incredible sufferings and persecutions Jews have undergone in the Christian West. The Church's various declarations asked forgiveness from the Protestants, the Eastern Orthodox, from the Moslems, but not from the Jews. Many Jews, especially those who lived through the Nazi holocaust, asked with great passion, 'How many more millions of our brothers and sisters will need to be slaughtered before any word of contrition or repentance is heard in the seats of ancient Christian glory?' " (Marc H. Tanenbaum, "A Jewish Viewpoint," in John H. Miller, ed., *Vatican II: An Interfaith Appraisal* [Notre Dame: Univ. of Notre Dame Press, 1966] p. 363). I may not be personally responsible for death on the hot sands of Sinai, for bloated bellies in Appalachia, for Southern laws that condemned blacks to illiteracy; but do I ever weep for them?

Remembrance and repentance call for conversion: I must change in mind and in heart. Here reconciliation becomes sticky. It is easy enough to deplore an individual sin, to say I shall try never to do it again. It is much harder to become the new person who does not act that way. It is relatively easy for me not to fire a gun, not to waste while a continent hungers, not to let bias destroy normal courtesy. It is ever so hard for me to become a man of peace, a man poor in spirit, a man who loves. But unless I do, I shall not become a force for reconciliation; I shall be one only with the few I like, the few who like me.

The radical break-through will come when I love God enough to love His every image on earth, when I see in every broken body, in all starved flesh, the crucified corpse of Christ. Only then will I do what Thomas Merton saw must be done: "our job is to love others without stopping to inquire whether or not they are worthy." Not with words only or primarily; all too many of us deny with our lives what we profess with our lips. We have reached that point in history where we either treat our neighbors as brothers and sisters or invite destruction.

In this connection, a Hasidic tale dear to the Jewish philosopher Martin Buber is splendidly pertinent: "A young student after much anguish knocked on the door of his rabbi. He cried out: 'Rabbi, I have eyes to see, ears to hear, and a mind to understand, yet I do not know for what purpose I was created or what meaning there is in my life.' The rabbi answered: 'Foolish one, neither do I know the purpose of existence, but come let us break bread together' " (cf. Arthur Gilbert, "The Contemporary Jew in America," *Thought* 43 [1968] 226).

V

Reconciliation Between Man and Nature

Recently the social philosopher and psychoanalyst Erich Fromm was interviewed by a New York newspaper. He had come to this country in the early 1930s, an exile from Hitler's Germany, hopes high for life and work in a vibrant America. Forty years later, he fears for his adopted country. "The United States is not yet entirely in hell. There is a very small chance of avoiding it, but I am not an optimist."

Why this gloom? One reason is what Fromm calls our "unrestrained industrialism." After World War II, America's industrial machine spewed an endless flow of motor cars and pleasure boats, refrigerators and air conditioners, barbecue pits and heated swimming pools. Such incredible excess of material things, Fromm claims, the machine process, has minified man, made his own life seem unimportant to him. "We have grown soft from it at a sacrifice of, what shall I call it, the soul." And, on the whole, we "have accepted the logic of machinery, which is to demonstrate how machinery works. The ultimate purpose of making a gun is to fire it."

In consequence, "America has become the world's most destructive society." Not only have we bombed Vietnam back to the Bronze Age. "Our society is also internally destructive. In the last decade or so, a million people have been killed in highway accidents. We produce cars with built-in obsolescence. Knowing the possible dangers, we continue to pollute the environment. And we subsidize violence on the screen—movies in which human life is depicted as brutish and cheap" (cf. New York Times, Dec. 15, 1973, p. 33).

I have analyzed three ruptures that call for reconciliation:

rupture between man and God, within man himself, between man and man. Now I take up a fourth facet of human disunity, a rupture Dr. Fromm has in mind, the rupture between man and nature, between man and things. I shall probe two problems: (1) what this rupture does to us, and (2) what this rupture asks of us.

1.

First, then, what is this rupture between man and nature? By "nature" I mean all that is not man or God. Till recently, you and I have pretty much taken nature, things, for granted. There they were—air and ocean, coal and natural gas, aluminum and oil, steer and salmon, wheat and milk and eggs, cars and boats and planes, drugs and electric lights—there they all were, in their natural state or the fruit of American know-how, at our disposal now and forever. Oh yes, much of it was hostile, had to be subdued; some of it belonged to others, had to be carried enslaved across continents; but when the chips were down, nothing could resist American ingenuity. What we wanted we could have. One tradition even boasted that such consistent success, such material prosperity, was a sign of God's election: we were a chosen people. All enemies would fall before our blessed might: not only ensouled peoples but the soulless soil, the bowels of the earth and the limits of outer space.

Suddenly all that changed. No longer could we take nature for granted. Each day a new headline horrified us, terrified us: "Last Pocket of Clear Air in United States Disappears"; "World Oxygen Level Threatened by Pesticides"; "Air Pollution Will Require Breathing Helmets by 1985"; "World Losing Water Pollution Battle despite Stepped-up Control Efforts"; "Chemical Fertilizers Called Threat to Water Resources"; "Millions Face Threat of Starvation"; "World Food Supplies Seen Running out by Year 2000"; "Experts Say Human Race May Have Only 35 Years Left" (Cf. Karl Menninger, *Whatever Became of Sin?* p. 121).

In fear, we looked at nature with new eyes, fresh awareness. I looked at human excrement pouring into the Hudson River, and I smelled not waste but death. I breathed deeply, coughed, and no longer found humor in the joke: "When does the snow get dirty in New York City? At ten thousand feet." I read that autos occupy more space in America than do people, and I felt strangled. I saw a tree felled in a few short moments, and I remembered that the tree had been centuries a-growing. I watched the Arab-Israeli crisis unfold, and realized that this winter our children and our aged might be cold, might freeze. I saw a lady look wistfully at chuck beef in a market, and the ceaseless surge in living costs became more than a statistic. I heard that, to power western cities, Navajo land would be strip-mined, and I thought of the horror that is Appalachia.

Appalachia. . . . Is it possible that Appalachia is, in miniature, America in the year 2000? "Every year Americans junk 7 million cars, 48 billion cans, 20 million tons of paper. Our industries pour out 165 million tons of waste and belch 172 million tons of fumes and smoke into the sky. We provide 50% of the world's industrial pollution. An average of 3000 acres of oxygen-producing earth a day (1,000,000 a year) fall beneath concrete and blacktop. The average American puts 1500 pounds of pollutants into the atmosphere each year. Furthermore, there is no end in sight" (Richard A. McCormick, S.J., "Notes on Moral Theology: April-September, 1970," *Theological Studies* 32 [1971] 97).

In all these facts and figures, what I find frightening is that we are enlarging the enmity that exists between man and his earth. It is as if we began with the curse of God in Genesis, "Cursed is the ground because of you" (Gn 3:17), experienced how reluctant nature often is to serve us, vowed that with our know-how and our power we rational creatures would enslave the irrational, and then carried our vow relentlessly to its logical conclusion. We have conquered the earth; it is subject, or soon will be, to our every will and whim. Only . . . the slave has turned on his master; cold reason is no longer in control; out of the nonhuman we have fashioned a monster, and the monster threatens to strangle us. The rupture that sin spawned, hostility between man and his environment, is reaching the point of no return. I can only hope that you are as frightened as I am.

2.

My second main point: what does this rupture ask of us? Obviously, reconciliation. But how do we achieve reconciliation? The answer is not easy, because the problem is complex; and the problem is particularly complex because it is not clear how we have come to this unpretty pass.

For some experts, we are where we are because of an American mentality, an American attitude, an American value system. We see the material world as a giant cookie jar. The world is a commodity and we are consumers. Since this life is either all there is or a vale of tears while we wait for a better life, it makes sense to raid the cookie jar. And so we profit, we pleasure, we pollute (Cf. J. Barrie Shepherd, "Theology for Ecology," *Catholic World 211* [1970] 172-75).

Other experts point to a dilemma that has confused American society since the nineteenth century: we worship nature, yet we exploit it. On the one hand, there is the religion of nature. Many work in the city while dreaming of the country; they work on supersonic transports and live in ranch houses to escape the city's noise. In communion with nature, they seek deity, virtue, vitality; finding God in the woods, they let the city stew in its sin. On the other hand, there is the religion of civilization. It was symbolized by the steam locomotive: we sang about it, its ability to leap rivers, grind rocks into powder, trample down hills. Here nature is "defined by its openness to manipulation and exploitation" (Cf. H. Paul Santmire, "Ecology and Schizophrenia: Historical Dimension of the American Crisis," *Dialog* 9 [1970] 175-92).

Others take us back a giant step. They blame our ecological crisis on the Christian understanding of the Old Testament. As they see it, the scientific stance of the Western world goes back to the first page of Scripture: "God created man in His own image, in the image of God He created him; male and female He created them. And God blessed them, and God said to them: 'Be fruitful and multiply, and fill the earth and subdue it; and have dominion over the fish of the sea and over the birds of the air and over every living thing that moves upon the earth' " (Gn 1:27-28). Subdue . . . dominion. Christianity (so the charge runs) sees in man the one center of the universe. All else—soil and sea and sky, blue marlin or bird of paradise, oil or coal or natural gas—all that is not man has for purpose, for destiny, to serve man, to serve his purpose, to serve his pleasure. Man is not part of nature; somewhat like God, he transcends nature. Man not only differs from the sub-human; the subhuman is his slave.

And Western man has lived his theology, has played his role of master, with a vengeance. In laboratory and forest, in factory and refectory, we pillage and we rape, we devour and we waste.

28

Why not? It is I who am God's image, master of all I survey—king of the earth (said some early Christian writers) as God is King of the universe. Man will be utterly one with nature only when "things" no longer resist man's will, no longer struggle against him.

Finally, a perceptive Protestant ethician, Joseph Sittler, insists that our basic ecological error is that we Christians have separated creation and redemption. The reason why we can worship nature in Vermont and at the same time manipulate nature in New York is because, in our view, the redemption wrought by Christ leaves untouched the creation wrought by God. And once we wrench redemption from creation, once we put nature out there and grace in here, as long as we omit from our theology of grace man's transaction with nature, it is irrelevant to Christians whether we reverence the earth or ravish it (Cf. Joseph Sittler, "Ecological Commitment as Theological Responsibility," Idoc, Sept. 12, 1970, pp. 75-85; also his remarks in John H. Miller, C.S.C., ed., Vatican II: An Interfaith Appraisal [Notre Dame: Univ. of Notre Dame Press, 1966] pp. 426-27).

Now each of these analyses says something important about man's rupture from nature, how that rupture came to be; and so each suggests in its own way how the rupture may be repaired, how man can be reconciled with his earth. But from all these analyses one word emerges as a critical corrective: responsibility. I am responsible for my earth. But if responsibility is to be real, is to lead to reconciliation, I must frame a fresh attitude to the earth, to all that is not human. How?

First, I dare not interpret the Genesis command "subdue the earth" to mean that God has given man unrestricted power to do with the earth whatever he will. God gives man not despotism but stewardship. And a steward is one who manages what is someone else's. A steward cares, is concerned, agonizes; he may not plunder or waste; he is responsible, can be called to account for his stewardship. "The earth is the Lord's" (Ps 24:1).

Second, we shall not be responsible stewards unless we shake off the consumer mentality: more things equals better persons. How difficult this is, the energy crisis reveals. We Americans, 6 percent of the world's population, have been consuming 30 percent of its energy. Our government's initial solution to the

29

sudden shortage? For a short time, sacrifice, less consumption. In the long run, how can we continue to consume 30 percent? Not *should* we, only how do it? Our spontaneous solution: Project Independence, the world as competition. Only later did we hear Project Interdependence, the world as community.

Third, we shall not be responsible stewards unless we sense the intimate unity, the inescapable solidarity, that links man to nature. We must take seriously the mystery-laden affirmation of St. Paul: when man in Christ is finally restored to his true nature and destiny, "the creation itself will be set free from its bondage to decay and obtain the glorious liberty of the children of God" (Rom 8:21). Man and his world are intended by God to grow together, to be redeemed together; they share a common destiny.

This means, fourth, an awareness that the subhuman is sacred. Everything that exists, from ocean floor to outer space, is precious because it reflects the God whose whole being is summed up in a monosyllable: He *is*. And everything that lives, from the simple amoeba through a field of wheat to the sulphur-bottom whale, is more precious still, because it images the God who *is* Life. Nature is sacred in its own right, even apart from man.

Responsible stewardship means, fifth, a realization that the earth belongs to *all* men. I do not deny your right to private property; but private property is not an absolute. It is subordinate to core personal rights: the right to life, to human dignity, to bodily integrity. America is not entitled to keep or consume everything it can produce or purchase. It is through the things of earth, from water to atomic energy, that man becomes human or inhuman; it is largely by his use of God's creation that man is saved or damned. And so it is frightening that two out of every five human beings fall asleep hungry each night; it is frightening that, despite the dollars pouring into Latin America, the rich get richer and the poor get poorer. Each man, each woman, each child have a strict right to as much of this earth's resources as they need to live a human existence in union with God. The earth is man's.

I have spent much space on attitudes, because only a new attitude can change America from rapist to steward. Only a fresh vision can change enemies into partners, reconcile man and his earth. But if love will not change us—love of God, of God's image, of God's creation—perhaps fear will. Raping the earth may destroy us, here and hereafter.

30

VI

Reconciliation:
Deeds Not Words

In this approach to reconciliation, my argument has been basically simple. I have argued that reconciliation implies rupture, a rupture on four levels: between man and God, within man himself, between man and man, between man and nature. I have argued that reconciliation, the destruction of rupture, ultimately comes through grace, through Christ, through love. And I have argued for fresh attitudes—to God, to myself, to my fellow man, to nature —new ways of looking at these realities, new ways of addressing them.

But attitudes and words are not enough. The Epistle of James is strong here: "Be doers of the word, and not hearers only" (Jas 1:22). And the First Epistle of John: "Little children, let us not love in word or speech but in deed and in truth" (1 Jn 3:18). The problem, of course, is: how?

A remarkable ecumenist, Lukas Vischer, made three reflections recently which he thought relevant for the Holy Year. He took from the Book of Leviticus, chapter 25, the three prescriptions of the ancient Jewish Year of Jubilee; each prescription suggested to him what *all* Christians might do so as to make 1975 more than a limited Catholic celebration (cf. *National Catholic Reporter*, Nov. 23, 1973, p. 11). The three prescriptions touch (1) ecology, (2) justice, (3) freedom. I should like to develop, to expand, his brief suggestions.

1.

One prescription fairly leaps out of Leviticus. The Lord says: "The land is mine; for you are strangers and sojourners with me" (Lv 25:23). The point is, the Jews were expected to "recognize this divine claim in each year of the sabbath and even more in each jubilee year. The land should rest in this year. The Jews should resist the temptation to regard the land as property to be manipulated by them. God's creation has its own right which has to be respected by us" (Vischer, *loc. cit.*).

What does this say to us today? I argued earlier that we Americans are raping the earth to our own destruction. We waste, we pillage, we pollute so prodigally that the earth we thought our slave has turned on its master, threatens to destroy us. I argued for a new attitude—against the consumer mentality, for a stance where we are not despots but stewards, aware of the intimate unity that links man to nature, aware that the subhuman too is sacred, aware that the earth belongs to *all* men.

With this new attitude, what must we do? First, we cut down on *waste:* we no longer "use, consume, or expend thoughtlessly or carelessly," no longer "use to no avail," no longer "squander" *(American Heritage Dictionary).* This means that many of us will eat less and drink less, smoke less and drive less, either wear the clothes we buy or give them to the poor, stop hoarding for an improbable future.

Second, we *pillage* less, plunder the earth with reluctance. Obviously, the earth cannot remain a sort of eternal Eden, virginal, untouched; man must live off the earth, is empowered to remake it. But I cannot believe that, with our technological know-how, each square foot of concrete must destroy a square foot of soil. I trust that the uncounted acres of Vietnam we have defoliated and depopulated we will help restore; this is not charity, this is justice. Those who hunt wildlife and shoot for sheer pleasure I do not ask to cease and desist; but I do ask them to examine their posture towards the subhuman: do they see the wild duck and the deer simply as man's plaything? The examples are legion, and each person has a different set of contacts with nature. But each of us should henceforth touch the "things" of God with greater reverence; where we must consume or destroy, let it be only because paradoxically it makes us more human.

Third, let us *pollute* only where pollution makes some measure of sense. Only where we can see pollution as a lesser evil. Only with a parallel effort to limit its destructiveness. The energy crisis compels us to temper our ideals, to come to terms with reality.

Please God, it will not mean compromising on principle: God's creation is sacred; touch it with reverence, pollute it with fear and trembling.

2.

A second prescription of the Jewish Year of Jubilee has the Lord commanding: "In this year of jubilee each of you shall return to his property" (Lv 25:13). The point is, "Those who have gone into debt and have had to sell their land shall have their land returned to them by the 50th year. As the land and all that it may produce is God's property, mankind should share it equally. The property should not be united in a few hands but should be for the benefit of the community" (Vischer, *loc. cit.*).

What does this say to us today? I argued earlier that we Americans need a new attitude towards those hundreds of millions in the world who do not live humanly. A graphic description of the problem caught my eye recently: "If the world were a global village of 100 people, 70 of them would be unable to read, and only one would have a college education. Over 50 would be suffering from malnutrition, and over 80 would live in what we call substandard housing. If the world were a global village of 100 residents, 6 of them would be Americans. These 6 would have half the village's entire income, and the other 94 would exist on the other half" (*IFCO News* 4/6 [Nov.-Dec. 1973] p. 12).

Such a desperate situation calls not only for an attitude; it calls for action. One example on the corporate level. The churches in this country are, in many instances, powerful operations. To operate efficiently, to help the needy, they invest in stocks and other securities. But the corporations in which churches invest are not merely tools for producing income; they have social consequences. By their policies, corporations may cause death, disease, injury—by decisions on pollution, plant safety, working conditions. They exercise influence and power, may even control and coerce—by propaganda, advertising, shady practices. Some corporations deal in death: napalm, poisonous gas, rockets. Some drain the resources of underdeveloped nations, while the rich in those nations get richer and the poor get poorer. Some assist racial policies by the support they give to racist governments.

The point is, the churches may no longer disregard the purposes to which their investments are put. They may not go along with a certain respected economist: "The question is, do corporate executives, provided they stay within the law, have responsibilities in their business activities other than to make as much money for their stockholders as possible? And my answer is that they do not. . . . The executive's job is to do whatever the shareholders would like to see done, and most of the time the shareholders only want to make money. . . . There is nothing that would in fact destroy the private enterprise system more than a real acceptance of the social responsibility doctrine" ("Milton Friedman Responds: A Business and Society Review Interview," *Business and Society Review*, Spring 1972, pp. 6-8, quoted by David Hollenbach, S.J., in *Theological Studies* 34 [1973] 268).

This, I submit, is unethical. Nothing is more destructive of humanity than rejection of social responsibility. The churches have a moral obligation (1) to know how their money is being invested, (2) to discover whether human beings are being injured or exploited by these investments, (3) to make value judgments on corporation policies, (4) to try to control unethical behavior in corporations, influence their policy, challenge their actions, and (5) in certain instances, to sell the stock they hold. The churches can be a unique force for social good. The effort to influence may be torturous—but so is death by starvation.

On the individual level, I must learn, perhaps for the first time, if my purchasing power, my purchasing habits, support injustice: to migrant workers, to minority groups, to the poor and the powerless. Problems of the immediate present such as lettuce and grapes are too complex to settle in a paragraph. The important thing is, you may not shut your eyes to what lies behind a head of lettuce or a bunch of grapes, just because it is all too complicated or you simply cannot be bothered. Human lives are at stake. And here enter my sins of omission. You know what agonizes me as I near life's late afternoon? I have written against injustice, preached against it, prayed against it; but I have never shouted against it, never linked arms with marchers for peace and justice, never laid my life on the line. It's always been behind a barricade; it's all been quite safe. And are you among those who told nuns to stay in their convents, stay out of Selma and Jackson? Are you among those who say that a priest's place is in the pulpit and not on a picket line? I'm afraid the theory is no longer Christian—if it ever was. Oh yes, some nuns and priests are quite stupid in the causes they espouse and the shibboleths they shout. But even at their worst they are aware that they are their brothers' keepers.

3.

A third prescription of the Jewish Jubilee Year: the slave was to be freed: "He shall be released in the year of jubilee, he and his children with him" (Lv 25:54). Our own jubilee year puts fresh pressure on Christians to press for freedom. First, we have sung the Star Spangled Banner so long and so thoughtlessly that we assume automatically America is "the land of the free." Not so.

A frightening number of Americans are slaves in the work they do. They are cogs in a machine. One half of their waking life is dull, monotonous toil which does not engage them as persons, is not what they want to do, does not show up in a product of which they feel a part, does not touch them to another human being, does not make them more human. A spot welder on the assembly line in an auto plant put it pungently: "They'll give better care to that machine than they will to you. If it breaks down, there's somebody out there to fix it right away. If I break down, I'm just pushed over to the other side till another man takes my place." The writer Studs Terkel summed it up: "Most of us, like the assembly line worker, have jobs that are too small for our spirit. Jobs are not big enough for people" ("Here I Am, a Worker," *New York Times,* March 19, 1973).

Many of you are employers. Are you among those employers who put an end to isolation by creating teams, who rotate jobs to ease monotony, who involve employees in decision-making, who use sensitivity training and encounter sessions so that workers get to know one another, who pay workers for continuing their education? Our economic system demands x-number of slaves. What are you doing to free them?

More than that: an increasing number of Americans are slaves because they have *no* work to do. They have no skills or their skills are not needed. And so they sit quietly or they stage sit-ins; they feel empty or they boil inside; they collect compensation for nothing and they agonize about tomorrow. And all the while they become less human: no contact with God's creation, no sense of being useful, just chained to a system that periodically promises

35

less unemployment—or so the statistics say. Do you *know* even one of these slaves? Does he make you uncomfortable? Do you even try to find work for him? One human person?

And in America about one of every twenty goes to bed aching from hunger. When was the last time you *did* anything about it? Something like 35,000 young Americans are exiles from our society because they could not in conscience support our Asian war. Is it Christian to demand that if they return, they be imprisoned? Is *this* our Holy Year?

Second, freedom is a demand not only on the world's most powerful country but on the world's most powerful Church. The Catholic Church in this Holy Year must free women to contribute their rich gifts to the ceaseless task of redeeming a world; they ought no longer be second-class citizens, with nothing to say in church or chancery, encouraged only to wash the linens of today's Church and the diapers of tomorrow's Church. And the Church must double its efforts to exercise authority as service and not as naked power, must recognize that religious obedience does not destroy human rights, must grasp anew how sacred is man's conscience even when in error. The Church is indeed the Body of Christ; and still the Church is not God.

Ultimately, no one else can define for you where your specific involvement lies. Knowing yourself and your situation, your gifts and your opportunities, you will grasp best what you can do. A dear friend of mine used to say: "I'm a brave man, but not a hero." Only the few are called to be heroes: a Solzhenitsyn challenging the tyranny of Russia, a Martin Luther King non-violently attacking white violence. But all of us are called to be brave: to look at the land, to look at persons, to look within us—and then to do . . . something. The Book of Isaiah says much in a short space when it puts these words on the lips of the Lord:

"Fasting like yours this day
will not make your voice to be heard on high. . . .

Is not this the fast that I choose:
to loose the bonds of wickedness,
to undo the thongs of the yoke,
to let the oppressed go free,
and to break every yoke?

36

Is it not to share your bread with the hungry,
  and bring the homeless poor into your house;
  when you see the naked, to cover him,
  and not to hide yourself from your own flesh?

Then shall your light break forth like the dawn,
  and your healing shall spring up speedily;
  your righteousness shall go before you,
  the glory of the Lord shall be your rear guard.

Then you shall call, and the Lord will answer;
  you shall cry, and He will say: Here I am."

(Is 58:4-9)